THE BOOK WE WISH WE HAD

Barstool revelations for building
a career in creative marketing

Jeremy Baka + Matt Molino

Published by River Grove Books
Austin, TX
www.rivergrovebooks.com

Distributed by River Grove Books

Design and composition by Curtis Pickell
Cover design by Greenleaf Book Group
Cover Images: ©Mega Pixel; Mariyana M. Used under license from Shutterstock.com

Publisher's Cataloging-in-Publication data is available.

Print ISBN: 978-1-63299-648-0

eBook ISBN: 978-1-63299-649-7

First Edition

To all the seasoned executives out there who despite being stressed out and busy as hell, still take the time to mentor the next generation of leaders.

Few amazing ideas ever unfold while sitting under fluorescent lights around a conference table or during a brainstorm with five tiny faces on a computer screen. Ideation is less scripted and messier than that.

Whether torturing a creative brief until it coughed up an idea, mocking industry work we wished we had created, breaking down the nuances of dark comedies, or just unpacking life's mysteries, we would inevitably find ourselves sitting alongside two well-crafted drinks. We admired the simple symmetry of great cocktails: equal parts spirits, citrus, and liqueurs. Too much of one or the other and the drink is ruined. The same can be said for the best ideas: equal parts strategy and creative. Or good mentors: equal parts supportive and straight talking. Or a great employee: equal parts thinker and doer.

That's how it flowed during our bar-storms. Sometimes, our ponderings culminated in thoughts so exciting we would write them up on the spot. Other times, ideas that seemed so brilliant after two martinis apiece looked like coded messages the following day, e.g., "Space water—nostalgia hook." WTF? One thing, however, remained consistent: No topic was ever too uncomfortable, no thought too strange, and no opinion too extreme. Everything was fair game in the creative octagon.

One night, as we discussed hard lessons learned, smart moves, and dumb decisions, we realized something—that is, something missing. All the business books of our day focus on the same usual suspects: leadership attributes, management skills, new marketing paradigms, and about a half-dozen other trampled topics. (Not including the anticipated flood of books about how to "navigate the new normal.") Respectfully, we concluded that the world didn't need another typical business book. What it needed was something real and raw, something higher education doesn't teach and companies don't train but everyone somehow expects you to know. A book so simple and pure, its purpose would be in the title: **The Book We Wish We Had.**

The Book We Wish We Had is less interested in how to hit a business home run and more fascinated by the game itself. It is a humble collection of in-the-trenches lessons obtained while working at some of the world's largest agencies and for some of the biggest brands on the planet, including Adidas, Apple, Amazon, Bank of America, Budweiser, Diageo, Ford, Hilton, Walmart, and more. It represents teachings learned the hard way, from being a boss to working for one, from failing miserably to achieving considerably, from mentoring to being mentored, from doing the wrong thing to discovering the right thing.

Following tons of riffing and sifting, the only bits of advice that made it into this book are those we believe will help make you more creative and business savvy. Consider it a business bible of sorts, featuring timeless truths that remain relevant even during global pandemics. The pages are to be read in no particular order, allowing you to experience the book in your own way. And we use the personal pronoun "I" throughout, choosing not to distinguish whether it's a Matt story or a Jeremy story. That's our way of reinforcing that the learnings within are perpetual, not generational.

So, if you're a senior executive who geeks out on business books that explore the kinetics of consumer behavior or deconstruct the latest marketing trends, this is definitely not the book for you. (Take heart, there are 100,000 such books on Amazon.) But, if you're a freshly-minted executive seeking a hidden edge in the form of business street smarts not offered at any college or dispensed during any company training, then this is your book. Your personal Tao of business. It won't take long for you to realize why this is **The Book We Wish We Had.**

Get a PhD in **people.**

I feel like I've earned two degrees in my life: one from Chapman University, the other from behind a bar–and the latter gave me a bigger return on my investment.

Working in quality restaurants and bars is like getting a PhD in people. It teaches you to listen and connect with people, to decipher verbal cues, decode body language, and read between the lines. (Research shows words account for only 7 percent of how we communicate. The rest is body language and tone of voice.)

It trains you to anticipate others' needs, diffuse difficult situations, and ultimately deliver a high-level service experience. I found joy in connecting with patrons at the bar, and I made it my personal mission to establish a deep and diverse network through these connections by building longer tables versus higher walls.

Be curious about people–*all* people–not just those who look like you. This opens you up to new voices and perspectives, allowing for more meaningful and deeper connections with those around you–something that will come in handy when attempting to connect with the biggest group of all: consumers.

Adopt a role model.

Olivet Nazarene University in Bourbonnais, Illinois, surveyed 3,000 people across 21 industries and found that 76 percent believe mentors are important, yet only 37 percent have one. Mentors are rarely down the hall, so don't limit yourself.

Role models can be inside or outside your work, close or unreachable, dead or alive—as long as they somehow push you, prod you, and incite you to be better. They serve as that internal muse urging you to do it, try it, experience it. For Jeremy, it's Doug Buemi, Steve Jobs, Pablo Picasso, Lin-Manuel Miranda, and former neighbor and charter-school teacher Eddie Doyne. For Matt, it's Jeremy Baka, Steve McQueen, Debbie Molino, Anthony Bourdain, Tinker Hatfield, and Kobe Bryant.

To find the right role model, step back and ask yourself: What do I admire most in people? In Doug Buemi, Jeremy saw integrity mixed with a rebellious attitude. Lin-Manuel Miranda was visionary and energizing. Eddie Doyne was a believer, *convinced* that inspiring forgotten kids could one day change the world. In Steve McQueen, Matt saw an approachable cool, while Debbie Molino displayed **courageous selflessness.** In Kobe Bryant, the Mamba Mentality.

Author and self-help guru Jim Rohn once proclaimed, "You are the average of the five people you spend the most time with, including yourself." Close. You are the *cumulation* of the five people you spend the most time with, including yourself. Mirror the right collection of adopted mentors, and the reflection you see will be anything but average.

A mentor is a **privilege**, not a right.

Mentorship is not an act of charity; it's an act of trust. No mentor is going to waste his or her time on someone who doesn't show any potential or takes their help for granted.

For a mentor, the mentee is an expression of themselves–a reminder of where they once were and the hard work (and help) it took to get where they are now. It's not about ego. It's about the unwritten law of wisdom among leaders: Pay it forward.

Remember, however, that mentorship is a two-way street. The mentor shares hard-earned secrets from years of hustle and unrelenting resolve, while the mentee must prove they are willing and worthy to receive it.

"I can only show you the door," says Neo's mentor, Morpheus, in *The Matrix*. "You're the one who has to walk through it."

Enthusiasm goes a long way.

Michael Eruzione, the captain of the famous "Miracle on Ice" U.S. Olympic hockey team, which defeated the Soviet Union team in the 1980 Winter Olympics, once admitted that he may not be the best hockey player on ice, but send him into a group of players fighting over a puck and "I'll come away with it."

There's something to be said about enthusiasm. And, sadly, millions have said it. Google "enthusiasm quotes" and you'll get nearly 30 million search results. The notion of enthusiasm has devolved into nothing more than poster-quotes on corporate walls and commercial fodder for motivational speakers. That aside, enthusiasm remains a powerful jump starter as you continue to work on other specific skills that take more time. You can begin showing enthusiasm right now. It is an easy and meaningful way to immediately differentiate yourself from the pack.

100 doors.

Imagine a room with 100 doors. Behind one of them is THE idea, that breathtaking, award-winning kernel of thought that is part miracle, part persistence. You have a mere 1 percent chance of finding it, but that golden idea is always worth waiting for.

Great ideas don't come quickly or easily. That's why they're rare. Most people settle on "easy ideas" they believe are brilliant, but everybody else has also quickly landed on that same thought. That's how you end up with 42 auto ads with yet another car racing through the 2nd Street tunnel in LA.

If you're satisfied with the idea you found behind door number 3, 10, or 25, just know that someone else out there is opening doors 26 through 100.*

How many doors are you willing to open?

*Shout-out to BCW Chief Creative Officer Fede Garcia for his 100-doors philosophy.

Your **favorite creative** might be in the finance department.

Kim was our super-sharp finance director who not only loved figuring out operational puzzles but was a creative talent too. It wasn't uncommon for us to tap her ingenious thinking during brainstorms.

One day, Kim mentioned that a client of ours, Tom, had an overpayment on an invoice that was still unresolved. Tom was a mid-level marketing guy who was standing in the way of us getting approval on an amazing campaign we had developed. One day, exasperated by another infuriating call with him, I let my frustration spill over while talking to Kim. I said, "Hey, here's a suggestion, Kim. When you send that email to Tom about his credit, include a note that says, 'Tom is a dick.'"

Kim pondered this for a moment, tilting her head and furrowing her brows. "What do I get if I do?" she asked.

"Lunch on me," I shot back. "For a week!" I added.

Later that day, Kim walked into my office and handed me a note she had sent to Tom. "You owe me lunch," she said, casually. It wasn't until I read the first letter of each sentence that I realized she had done it.

That kind of creativity was worth every penny of every lunch.

Hi Tom,

Time to revisit this credit again . . .

Once more, there is a credit of $17,842.00 on our books.

Most of the current invoices are still unpaid (with many that are 61–90 days past due).

I know you were going to discuss with Phillis on how to proceed. We would like to resolve this as soon as possible.

So, any direction on how to apply the over-payment would be appreciated.

As I recall from our phone conversation, you would rather not receive a refund check.

Does this still hold true?

I hope all is well with you.

Cheers,
Kim

"Yes, how can I help?"

These five words were recommended by a colleague of mine to her 22-year-old son when he scored a coveted internship at HBO. “When anybody asks you anything ever,” she explained, “you respond with five words: ‘Yes, how can I help?’” He is now a senior executive at a pay television network.

When starting out, say “yes” to everything no matter how menial or major. Become the person everyone turns to when they want something done right and with great enthusiasm. (See what we did there?)

Just as important as saying “yes” is asking “how.” Asking how you can help affords an opportunity for more insight and understanding around the challenge, allowing you to jump in in the most productive and expeditious way possible.

Turning down assignments, claiming you’re too busy, or waiting around to be told what to do is the fastest path to hearing another five words: “Sorry it didn’t work out.”

The backroads of **Bentonville.**

In the first three months of my career, the Los Angeles agency where I worked was on a deadline to develop final boards for a presentation to Walmart in Bentonville, Arkansas. With less than a day to spare, the only way the boards were going to reach the pitch team on time was if someone hand-delivered the package.

And that someone would be me, the new guy.

On August 31st, I was selected to race the boards to LAX, hop on a flight to Denver, grab a puddle jumper to Tulsa, and drive straight through the night to Bentonville. I made the handoff at 5 a.m. the next day, and then turned around and headed back. We ultimately won the assignment.

No one at work knew August 31st was my birthday and that my plans for the evening had been shattered. On the other hand, I earned a reputation as a go-to guy who could get the job done. Of course, rather than heading to Bentonville, I could have said, "Hey guys, I would really love to help but unfortunately it's my birthday and I have plans tonight." They would have understood, I'm sure. But it would have been a missed opportunity to show my dedication and determination to help the company win. It was an early turning point in how my team and the agency viewed me. I was the guy who took every request, every brutal assignment, every menial task, and ran with it–even on my birthday.

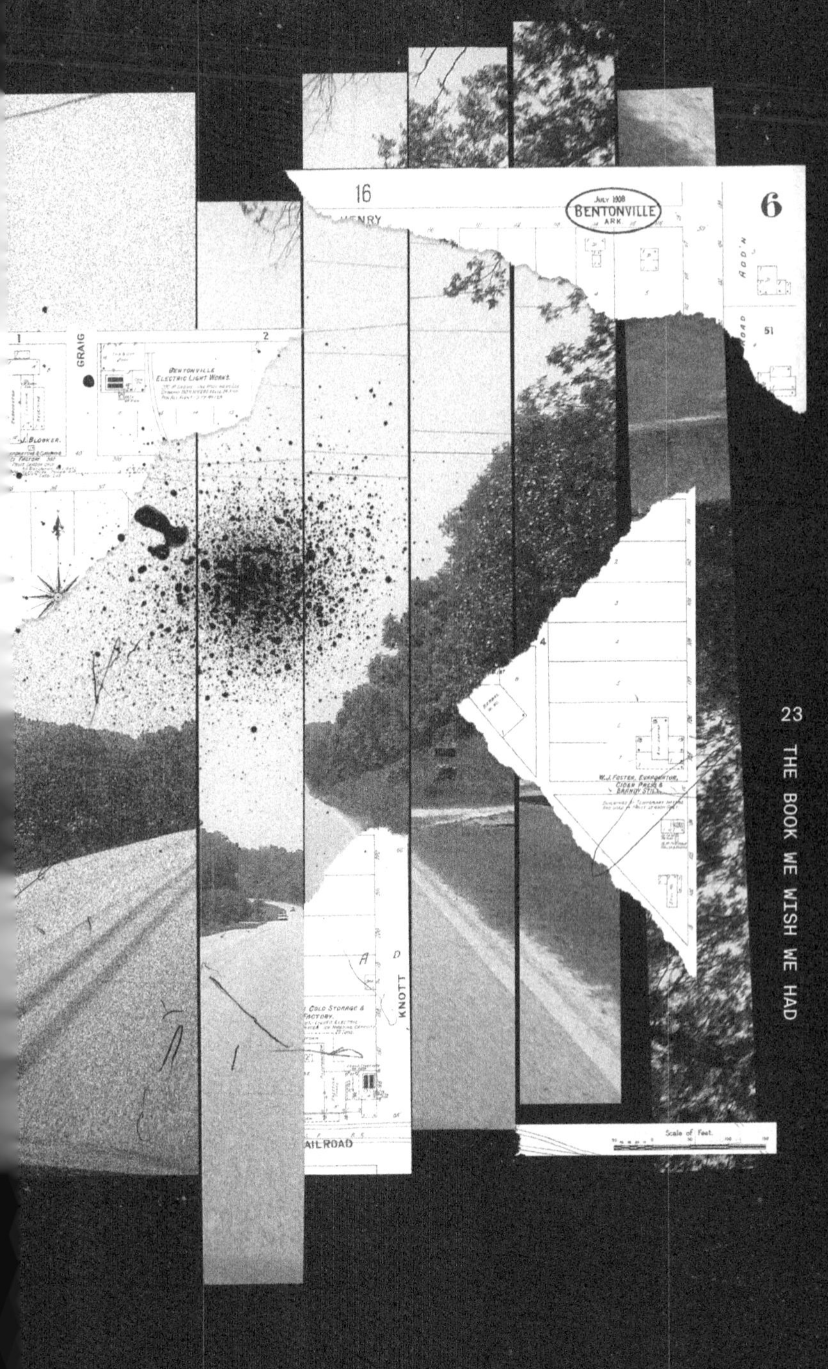
16
JULY 1908
BENTONVILLE
ARK
6
HENRY
ADD'N
ROAD
51
GRAIG
BENTONVILLE
ELECTRIC LIGHT WORKS
J. BLOOKER
W.J. FOSTER, EVAPORATOR,
CIDER PRESS &
BRANDY STILL
KNOTT
COLD STORAGE &
FACTORY
AILROAD
Scale of Feet

Exploit your passions.

Every damn one of them.

Casual conversations with bosses and work peers are a great opportunity to share your outside passions and interests. Even in today's remote-work environment, companies still have mixers and group gatherings online where people are encouraged to interact and team build.

Don't be afraid to share hobbies or nerd out about offbeat things. Not only does this create a deeper connection with colleagues, but you would be surprised how often spontaneous discussions like these lead to new opportunities for you. (As a young exec, Matt's obsession with sneaker culture lead to a prominent role on an Adidas pitch, while Jeremy's love of independent filmmaking lead to video production gigs for clients.)

Your hobbies and interests also enable you to emerge as a natural expert at work. From cooking to cars, music to makeup, or fashion gowns to fishing gear, the more personal passions you can bring, the more fun work will be and the more uniquely valuable you become.

Don't be **irrelevant.**

Saying nothing during meetings, calls, or discussions makes it seem like you have nothing worthy to offer or contribute. Do that often enough and your boss, clients, and colleagues will soon conclude it's true.

No matter how scary or draining speaking up may feel, get your voice out there. (That means you too, introverts.) Self-professed introvert Susan Cain, author of the best-selling book *Quiet: The Power of Introverts in a World That Can't Stop Talking*, has this suggestion for those who may be reticent about speaking up: "Figure out what you are meant to contribute to the world and make sure you contribute it. If this requires public speaking or networking or other activities that make you uncomfortable, do them anyway. But accept that they're difficult, get the training you need to make them easier, and reward yourself when you're done."

Start practicing now–testing, exploring, experimenting with how to positively and convincingly frame up or defend your thinking, opinions, and ideas. The more you practice, the better you become. So when the time comes–and it will–you will be well-rehearsed in thinking on your feet in front of the client.

Keep these two things in mind: 1) Silence leads to invisibility. 2) No one in the agency business has ever been fired for saying the wrong thing in a meeting. At least not in our combined 40 years in business.

Be heard or be forgotten.

I was once in a meeting with two junior colleagues and a client from an online music-sharing company. The discussion centered on how to get young, twentysomething musicians to use their product as a music-collaboration platform. **We spoke for nearly two hours about the feelings, attitudes, opinions, lives, and behaviors of young musicians.**

After the client left, I called the two junior colleagues into my office to get their thoughts on the meeting and the things discussed. The two budding executives shared their thinking about music-sharing platforms, friends who were musicians, things that might work, others that might not, and more. "Excellent," I said. "Why didn't you share any of that thinking in the meeting?" They stared at me blankly. Despite being in the same age group as the audience the client was targeting, both had sat silently in the room. "Your presence in that meeting was irrelevant," I explained. "It's almost as if you weren't there at all." I knew my comment stung, but I also never wanted them to forget it.

Years later, after both colleagues had moved on, I received an email from one of them who had gone on to be a successful executive at another agency. The subject line read: "I Was Not Irrelevant Today." In her email, my former colleague explained that although it was difficult to hear at the time, my comment pushed her to strive never to be irrelevant again. "I always try to add something valuable," she wrote. "Or at least follow-up with a compelling thought or observation." She went on to say she even had the "relevance conversation" with a young new hire at her company.

Let the relevance revolution begin.

Know what you want.

What do you want to do? What would get you out of bed each morning and whistling your way to work? If you can't figure that out, you're in for a potentially unsatisfying and unfulfilling career. So make a decision. If you know and you've decided what you want but aren't doing it, act on it now.

Don't stay in the wrong job (or career) simply because it's difficult, uncomfortable, or scary to go somewhere else. The longer you wait, the more you narrow your job experience and increase your salary, which makes it harder to jump careers at a similar pay scale.

And don't eliminate the possibility that you might just be able to create your dream job at the place you are now. Be clear in reviews about where your interests lie and what you want to do. Be vocal about it with colleagues and coworkers. Whenever possible, look for opportunities to get involved in your area(s) of interest. If you like the creative end of business, ask to be a part of creative discussions or brainstorms, volunteer for creative assignments—even if that means working weekends.

The more you love what you do, the less it seems like work.

DNFU* lunch.

No matter what you're doing, do it like a promotion depends on it. Regardless of how menial or unimportant you may think the task or assignment is, to somebody out there, it's important. What's more, doing the simplest task wrong or with a bad attitude makes you look incompetent or entitled.

Al Tortorella, considered a pioneer of today's corporate crisis management practice, once said, "If you want to know how good an entry-level hire is going to be, have them take the lunch order. If they care enough to get the sandwiches right, they've got potential."

*DNFU—"Do Not Fuck Up"—is an acronym made famous by the front-of-house team at the iconic Studio 54 New York nightclub in the late '70s. It was the unwavering philosophy behind the club's VIP-level treatment, which became the gold standard of service. Every guest is treated like a VIP—because most think they are.

Be an obnoxious connoisseur of **culture** and **content.**

Know stuff. Lots of stuff. But don't be a know-it-all. There's a difference.

A breadth of knowledge gives you something everyone, especially creatives, needs: a databank full of new, old, weird, meaningful, useless, profound, quirky, smart, and fascinating information. You'll never know when some piece of knowledge you possess will miraculously combine with something random to create something extraordinary.

In 2008, while browsing a bookstore for a "big fat book to read on vacation," Lin-Manuel Miranda famously settled on the 818-page biography *Alexander Hamilton*. "By the end of the second chapter," Miranda recalls, "I was furiously on Google saying, 'How has no one written a hip-hop musical about this man?'" Seven years later, the Broadway musical *Hamilton* became a pop-culture phenomenon, racking up a record-shattering 16 Tony Award nominations. (See: *Read*)

Absorb everything. Be aware of what is happening not just in *your* world, but in *the* world, from fashion to food, sports to space, pop culture to top news, business interest to human interest. Read things you usually wouldn't, watch shows you haven't, listen to people you've ignored, walk in someone else's shoes. Broadcast journalist Barbara Walters once declared, "I can get a better grasp of what is going on in the world from one good Washington dinner party than from all the background information NBC piles on my desk."

In the end, your ability to navigate a wide range of topics helps differentiate you in all settings and situations, from broad discussions and strategy sessions to brainstorms and dinner parties.

Read.

Read ravenously and relentlessly—magazines, books, blogs, blurbs, posts, news sites, cereal boxes, anything. Just read. According to a *Fast Company* survey, CEOs read an average of 60 books per year. That's about a book a week. And Tom Corley, author of the book *Change Your Habits, Change Your Life*, reports that nearly 90 percent of the self-made millionaires he interviewed read at least 30 minutes a day. If you're not reading, you're not learning.

Business magnate Warren Buffet said it best: "Reading is how knowledge works. It builds up like compound interest."

Reading fills your brain with simmering kernels of knowledge just waiting for the heat of a wandering thought to pop an idea into your head.

Neuroscientists explain that the brain continues to subconsciously work on a problem even after we step away from it. As we relax or fall into routine behaviors, the mind begins to wander, making remote and unexpected synaptic connections. It's no accident that "aha moments" seem to occur while walking, driving, showering, or drifting off to sleep. That's the result of the brain's neurons slamming into each other like bumper cars, giving you a rush of excitement when a connection is made. So, all of that stuff you're reading now—from unfinished rap lyrics to a book on a historical figure in politics—may not mean anything right now, but someday it might become *Hamilton*.

Change your **pronoun.**

Always celebrate the we, not the *me*.

If you consistently hear yourself saying, "I developed a program" or "My client is happy," perhaps it's time to change your pronoun, from I/me/my to we/us/ours.

We won the business.

We developed the concept.

We look forward to your thoughts.

Not only is "I" talk self-aggrandizing, but it also erroneously suggests that one person is singularly responsible for all the thinking on the team. Clients need to have confidence in the whole team, not just in you. It's a multiplayer game, not solitaire. And that also means no finger-pointing when things go south. We succeed or fail—as a team.

(See: *You Don't Demand Loyalty, You Demonstrate It*)

Balance isn't a recipe.

Show people they can count on you whether you're in the office or out. Keep a peripheral eye on emails during weekends, holidays, and vacations, just in case someone needs you. Let them know your commitment goes beyond the 9-to-5, Monday-through-Friday mentality. No, it's not always convenient, but opportunity doesn't schedule its knock.

Legendary record producer Jimmy Iovine tells a story about working as a young production assistant at New York's famous Record Plant studio. On Easter Sunday 1973, the owner of the studio called and asked Iovine to come in to answer the phones.

"I'm Italian, I'm Catholic, I'm from Brooklyn," said the now-famous record producer. "My mother thought it was a bad idea. But I went anyway. I was like, 'I'll do anything.'" As it turns out, the studio head was just testing Iovine. He wanted to see how committed the novice producer was to his job. The owner was so impressed, he arranged to have Iovine meet John Lennon and help produce his next album—an early turning point in the ambitious producer's career.

If you're in search of work-life balance, you're in for a frustrating and never-ending quest. Neither work nor life is *ever* balanced, independently or together. There are bad days and good days in each, with one or the other always demanding more time than the other. Attempting to perfectly balance them is like using a measuring cup on a roller coaster. Life is not a measuring scale; it's a chess board with one hundred thousand quadrillion vigintillion different moves, decisions, urgent responses, and immediate opportunities that surface as the game unfolds, each with their own advantages and implications.

Balance isn't a recipe; it's a process.

If you're going to miss a deadline, **be proactive about it.**

Deadlines are like ocean waves on a windy day—**they keep coming until one eventually gets you.**

It's impossible to predict all the storms that might hit and cause delays on a project. But deadlines aren't missed overnight. Like hurricanes, there are warning signs—dark clouds, gathering winds and rain—that suggest something isn't going as planned. Read the signs, and get in front of it.

After trying to manage the situation on your own, let your boss or client know as early as possible that you're likely to miss the deadline. Depending on how critical the deadline is, you may be able to move it without any real repercussions. (A formal presentation date is different than the deadline for a periodic update report.) Explain the unexpected situation and all that you've done to course correct. Most importantly, have a plan of action and a proposed new deadline. Then, do **not** miss the revised date.

Note: Deadline extensions should be used sparingly. Agreeing upon a realistic deadline in the first place will go a long way toward avoiding the need for deadline extensions. Better to request more time now than beg for it later.

Good work begets more work.

NFL running backs who average 90+ yards a game subsequently get more touches of the ball. Makes sense. The better you are at your job, the more work (opportunities) you get. Pick any sport. In every instance, players who perform the best play the most. In the NBA, for example, players with the most playing time in league history include Kareem Abdul-Jabbar, Bill Russell, Karl Malone, Michael Jordan, Kobe Bryant, Reggie Miller, and LeBron James.

The better you perform, the more will be demanded from you. That's the way it works. In fact, if your boss or team is *not* consistently throwing you the ball and demanding you score, you might want to ask yourself why.

It's always better to have your number called than remain on the bench.

(See: *Don't Be a Chump*)

Write amazing sentences.

As the legend goes, Ernest Hemingway, known for his terse copy and clipped prose, once bet a group of writers he could write a story using just six words. He wrote: "For sale. Baby shoes. Never worn."

Whether crafting copy to bring an idea to life or sending an update email to a client, commit to writing great sentences. Your writing style says as much about you as your fashion style. Do you want to be seen as smart, savvy, and sharp, or banal, bumbling, and boring? Kill the clichés. Junk the jargon. Write tight. No one wants to read thoughts, ideas, or language that feel stale.

Begin by writing a stirring first sentence that makes people want to read more. Prolific novelist Stephen King takes days, weeks, even months to craft the perfect first sentence for his books. "It's the first thing that acquaints you, that makes you eager, that starts to enlist you for the long haul," explains King. "There's incredible power in it, when you say, come in here, you want to know about this, and someone begins to listen." On the other hand, he emphasizes, "A really bad first line can convince me not to buy a book, because, God, I've got plenty of books already."

Set the tone with that first sentence and then make sure the rest of the copy lives up to it.

“FOR SALE. BABY SHOES. NEVER WORN.”

ERNEST HEMINGWAY

It takes guts to be the odd person out.

Whether in casual discussions or decision-making meetings, it can be tempting to just go along with what everyone else is saying or what others believe, especially if you don't have the same years of experience.

Be bold and brave enough to state your opinion and defend it–even if it goes against the grain. Making a convincing argument for your position shows strength, confidence, and conviction. People will even respect you for it–as long as you make a salient point or argument. Be prepared to feel the heat of embarrassment if you're just winging it. There's a difference between having an opinion and a good opinion. The latter requires the knowledge to back it up.

Steve Jobs was an asker. At age 12 he called Bill Hewlett, co-founder of Hewlett-Packard, and asked him for some spare computer parts. (Hewlett's home phone number was actually in the phone book back then.)

Not only did Hewlett agree, but he offered the young go-getter a summer job. As Jobs explained years later, "I've never found anyone who's said no or hung up the phone when I called. I just asked. Most people never pick up the phone and call, most people never ask. And that's what separates, sometimes, the people that do things from the people that just dream about them."

Wondering why you weren't picked for that open role at the company? Want more exciting assignments at work? Curious about working in an office overseas? Ask. If you don't, it's 100 percent certain you will never know.

Consider this: If someone had a hundred dollar bill and said, "If you ask me the right question, I'll give it to you," would you at least give it a shot, asking something, anything? Why wouldn't you? Nothing is at stake. If you lose, you just go about your day. Don't let doubt, fear, or pride keep you from the experience of a lifetime or an extraordinary business opportunity. If the answer is "no," the only thing hurt is your ego.

(See: *Ego Kills*)

Don’t be in a rush to **get it wrong.**

In today's "be first or forget it" business environment, no one ever has time to do it right, but everyone has time to do it over. Don't be afraid to push pause, even if everyone else is pressing fast-forward. Being first has no value if you're merely the first to arrive in the wrong place.

Harold Burson, the godfather of modern-day public relations, once shared a story about the CEO of a major steel company who came to him with an urgent request. Employee satisfaction scores at the company were plummeting, and the CEO wanted to host an extravagant Employee Appreciation Day, complete with games, bands, rides, and more. "I want our people to know we appreciate everything they do," declared the CEO.

Before rushing to execute the grand affair, Burson asked for one small thing: research. The CEO begrudgingly agreed. A week later, the results were in. The real cause of employee dissatisfaction? Parking. Employees were frustrated with the lack of parking spaces at the ever-expanding company. Many were forced to park far away and walk long distances in the rain and snow to get to work. Forget the festival games, employees were mired in their own game of parking-spot musical chairs. Burson worked with the company to introduce new parking guidelines, and employee satisfaction soon went back up.

Like so many splashy marketing campaigns, the Employee Appreciation Day would have been the most exciting and unforgettable event ever to not solve a problem.

The game will slow down.

Like athletes, when you first start playing at a pro level, everything seems to be moving insanely fast. But the more you play, the more you hone your skills and the more manageable the game seems. Suddenly, you can almost predict what will happen next.

Researcher and psychologist Mihaly Csikszentmihalyi calls this state of mind "flow." It's a state in which "the ego falls away. Every action, movement, and thought follows inevitably from the previous one," explains Csikszentmihalyi. "Like playing jazz. Your whole being is involved, and you're using your skills to the utmost."

To increase your chances of "flow," avoid getting too caught up in the outcome. Just stay in the moment, focused on creating the best campaign, the best presentation, the best event possible. Admittedly, this isn't as easy as it sounds, with the client, your boss, your team, and a host of others demanding your attention. Take a deep breath, summon all your skills, and take it one challenge at a time.

(See: *If You're Going to Miss a Deadline, Be Proactive About It* and *Be an Asker*)

Leave perfect scores to **egotistical assholes.**

The "360 review" is a standard business-performance evaluation process. Along with the company gathering input from those you work for or with, this sort of review also invites you to assess your own achievements and shortcomings. But how do you do both without looking arrogant or weak?

Unless you wear sandals and can walk on water, stay away from giving yourself a string of perfect scores. There's always room for improvement. Better for your reviewer to think you deserve a higher score than for them to think you're either clueless or too full of yourself. Be honest about where you think you can improve. This shows confidence, trust, integrity, and self-awareness. In other words, send the message that you're good, but looking to become even better.

Most importantly, set your ego aside and be honest with yourself. Do you really think you're doing a great job compared to others in your peer group at the company? If not, give yourself the highest grade you feel is defendable along with the steps you plan to take to get better.

The two **fuck yous** of business performance.

There were times in my career when I had to put people on probation for poor performance. I often explained at the end of these difficult reviews, "You now have two choices, and both involve the phrase 'Fuck you.' You can say, 'Fuck you, I'm out of here,' or, 'Fuck you, I'll show you.' Which is it going to be?" Most chose the former. A proud few chose the latter–and showed us what they were capable of.

Pick one.

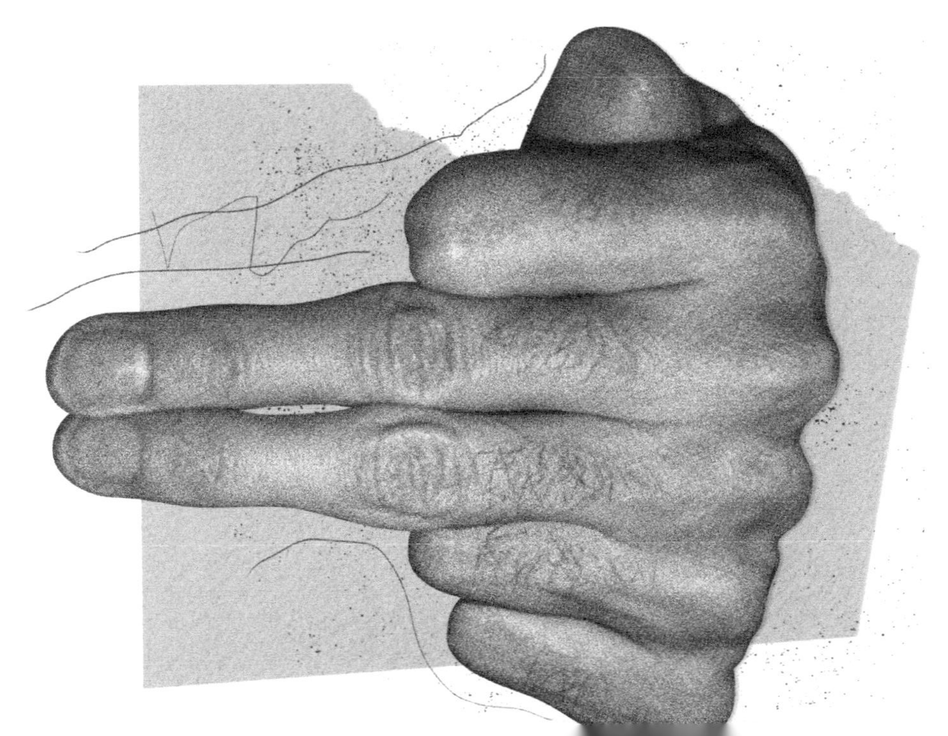

Not an **agency guy.**

I would have never guessed that in the second month of my first marketing job I would be on the chopping block. I was thankful to have finally gotten the call for this entry-level communications gig, just before the growing recession resulted in a hiring freeze at the firm. I was the agency's freshest hire.

Just eight weeks in, I was invited to join members of the senior team for drinks after work. I was filled with nervous excitement. As I sat bantering and drinking cocktails with the group, I began feeling more and more a part of the team. Before long, I found myself standing next to Deborah, the head of the office. Noticing me next to her, she pulled me aside. As a rookie, I was eager to pick up any pearls of wisdom from this seasoned pro. Instead, she took a hard look at me and said, coldly, "I'm not sure you're an agency guy."

I wasn't sure if I heard her correctly, or even what that meant, so I leaned in closer as she continued. "You have a way with people and are a hard worker," she conceded, "but you don't have the formal communications experience we need. This industry might not be for you." I stood there awkwardly nodding, too shocked to speak. Welcome aboard. You're fired.

I hadn't even gotten my business cards and already I was on probation. I had tried so hard to get up to speed quickly, handle the daily flood of work, and be the first person in the office each day (even though I lived two hours away)—had I already blown it? I felt sick. I spent the long drive home retracing my last several weeks and trying to estimate how far I could stretch my next and last paycheck.

The next day, I confided my worries in two senior people I felt I could trust. With their help, along with my own determination, I doubled down. I continued to work on my marketing fundamentals. I made sure to go above and beyond, wherever, however, and for whomever possible. As best I could, I made myself invaluable, resolving to use that as my protective shield against any pending axe. And . . . I also got lucky. We were pitching a spirits brand, the perfect chance to showcase my bartending experience and spirits knowledge while helping the team shine. Suddenly, I was being pulled into key meetings, asked for my advice, and invited to share ideas. I was soaring. My confidence was back and so was my career.

Upon reflection of that whole experience, I realized something. While I might not have been Deborah's agency guy, I was certainly someone's. And those someones who believed in me, trusted in my abilities, and helped me learn made me an even better agency guy as I rose into a leadership position.

Think for them when they don't have time.

More than all the surveys, studies, interviews, and stories about the attitudes, behaviors, and opinions of top executives, the *Wall Street Journal* summed up in three words what CEOs need most: "Time to think."

Particularly when society, business, and the world are undergoing tectonic shifts, CEOs are buried in status reports, operational upheaval, troubleshooting, planning, legal concerns, marketing pivots, shareholder demands, and a list of other urgent issues that compete for their mental bandwidth. That's where you come in.

Don't just think *like* them, think *for* them. Make proactive thinking your distinguishing trait. No matter if you're a CEO running a Fortune 500 company or a new hire fresh out of college, being able to see around corners makes you invaluable.

Don't just collect the dots, connect the dots. Find an unexpected angle, bring a fresh perspective, share a new direction that everyone else missed because they're too close to the situation or too distracted.

Sometimes, just taking the initiative can raise your worth and earn you a seat at the decision-makers table. For example, share some research you did on a topic the team was wondering about at a prior meeting.

Showcasing your critical thinking can make you a critical part of the team.

There's a difference between client service and **client servitude.**

Once while working on a big account as a mid-level manager, I was determined to not only keep the business but grow it. I worked 24/7, treating every client request as if it were handed down on stone tablets. If my client wanted a partnership with a charity, I arranged it. If he wanted to form a think tank, I put it together. If he wanted a campaign for the holidays, I created it. I was hitting it out of the park. What could go wrong?

A few months later, the client fired us.

As curious as I was baffled, I called him to ask what I could have done better. "I took every idea you had and ran with it," I said to him. "I did everything you suggested." He readily agreed with that assessment, but promptly added, "That was the problem. I was doing all the thinking."

You don't get extra-credit points delivering your boss or a client exactly what they requested. Waiters and waitresses do that too. Surprise them. Deliver something they didn't think to request or never imagined. (We once turned a $1,500 photo shoot into an international news-driving opportunity.)
(See: *Miracle on Rodeo*)

It's also worth noting that bosses and clients are not all-knowing, infallible, enlightened, or divine. They can be mistaken, ill-informed, or flat-out wrong. Going along with everything they say just to keep them happy or to protect your job is not only reckless and cowardly, but it also shows you have no confidence in your own skills and experience.

It's easy for a boss or client to find another waiter or waitress. It's tough to find another smart, creative mind with an intriguing thought or opinion.

Don’t be a **chump.**

There's a difference between criticism and abuse. Criticism is constructive in that being made aware of your strengths and weaknesses is an essential part of gaining a deeper understanding and long-term career growth. Abuse is different. It demeans you, demoralizes you, and destroys your self-respect.

Never let a boss or client publicly curse, trash, or degrade you. If you repeatedly let that happen—especially in public—you not only lose their respect and your own, but also that of your team. And if people don't respect you, why would they ever respect your opinions? That doesn't mean, however, becoming thin-skinned when someone is simply being assertive or direct with their feedback. There's a difference.

My friend and mentor Doug Buemi once took a stand against a client who was so abusive no one wanted to work on the business. As the company owner, Doug had finally had enough. "In the words of the great E. E. Cummings," he defiantly announced to the client on that glorious day, "there is some shit I will not eat." We lost the lucrative account, but Doug gained mad respect from everyone at the agency. It was a clear message: A demanding client is a natural part of doing business. An abusive client isn't worth the business.

Be a creative distillery, **not a creative factory.**

Trying to impress the client with how many ideas you can instantly crank out is like trying to impress the police with how fast you can drive. It doesn't serve your purpose.

Spitting out ideas like a gumball machine cheapens what you do. What's more, it reinforces the worse possible myth about the idea process: that it's fun and easy.

Great ideas require endless cogitation, consideration, exploration, discussion, and dissection. And when you're done . . . you start all over again. Ideas take time. You're not just turning a dial for some colorful gumballs; you're mining an entire mountain for rare and magnificent diamonds.

Jealousy and envy are underrated.

Anyone even remotely driven who says they never get jealous at seeing someone else reach new heights is either lying or delusional.

Gates vs. Jobs. Magic vs. Bird. Biggie vs. Tupac. Evert vs. Navratilova. Madame Curie vs. every male scientist of the early 20th century. There is ample evidence of how a healthy desire to be better than the next person makes us better.

"We were competitive, yeah," recalls Paul McCartney about his writing partner John Lennon. "He would say, 'Hmm, that's a bit good, right, here we go, come on.' If he'd have written 'Strawberry Fields,' [Forever], I would write, ' Penny Lane .'"

Seeing amazing creative work that isn't ours is like congratulating your best friend who just stole your girlfriend.

Upon hearing a great idea from someone in a brainstorm, a funny, smart, contagiously effusive former colleague of ours, we'll call her Eva, would jokingly say, "Oh my God, that's *brilliant.* I just want to punch you in the face right now!" The room would erupt with laughter. (Postscript: After leaving our company, Eva used her wonderfully wicked catchphrase at her new agency and was promptly ordered to take sensitivity training. Buzz kill.)

Obsess over, worship, hate, and revere work that makes you jealous or envious. Then, harness that energy to go create something better.

Brainstorms are not designed to **solve problems.**

Don't expect brainstorms to magically solve your problem between 2 p.m. and 3 p.m. Brainstorms are not about finding "the answer" but about facilitating a steady stream of creative consciousness, where obscure thoughts, impossible notions, and seemingly unrelated connections are explored. Afterward, you can discuss which ideas might best solve your problem, but doing that during a brainstorm will only kill the flow of ideas and decrease the creative output, as each idea is relentlessly vetted, analyzed, assessed, and critiqued.

More importantly, you never know where an offbeat comment or seemingly ridiculous idea might lead. Ben Steele, Chief Creative Officer at the outdoor recreation retail store REI, recalled a brainstorm where they were seeking a breakthrough holiday campaign. "We would never do it," one participant joked, "but what if we closed on Black Friday?" That year, REI launched #OptOutside, closing its stores and website during the coveted Black Friday sales period, encouraging people to go outside instead. The campaign captured worldwide attention and doubled membership and sales.

If your brainstorms are consumed with finding the "right" answer, you'll have no shot at ever landing on the more extraordinary one.

Unleash the **introverts.**

Be sure quieter colleagues are heard and get a chance to share their thoughts and ideas. Temper the extroverts, when necessary, to make space for other new and different voices in the room. Otherwise, the only perspectives you'll be getting are from those willing to shout the loudest. "Any time people come together in a meeting, we're not necessarily getting the best ideas, we're just getting the ideas of the best talkers," cautions Susan Cain, author of the *New York Times* best-selling book *Quiet: The Power of Introverts in a World That Can't Stop Talking*.

Consider approaches that allow introverts to more easily participate in meetings or brainstorms, such as inviting people to share their ideas via the chat window during online calls. Also, allow time for "solo storming," where, prior to a brainstorm, everyone ideates on their own and emails their ideas to a facilitator ahead of time. The facilitator then shares everyone's ideas with the broader group, inviting people to build on them. Giving equal space to all gives you a better chance of gathering the best ideas . . . not just the loudest.

“QUIET PEOPLE HAVE THE LOUDEST MINDS.”

STEPHEN HAWKING

Committees are cul-de-sacs.

British parliamentary official Sir Barnett Cocks once observed, "A committee is the cul-de-sac down which ideas are lured and then quietly strangled." Treat committees like kids treat broccoli–partake if you must, but do your best to avoid them.

Being on a committee makes everyone feel like they must contribute, and people end up offering opposing opinions, expressing concerns, and overengineering everything. With all that input, the result is often a Frankenproject–a hodgepodge of conflicting ideas, thoughts, and recommendations crammed together in an impractical way.

Before establishing that slow-moving, cumbersome committee, consider instead just pulling together one or two people. Do some collective thinking around the project and plan out how you wish to approach it. Once your idea is well formulated, get one-on-one feedback from other invested individuals–not groups of people–and use the feedback you think makes sense. By the time you present your project to the broader decision-maker(s), it will already have the tacit approval and feedback of key players.

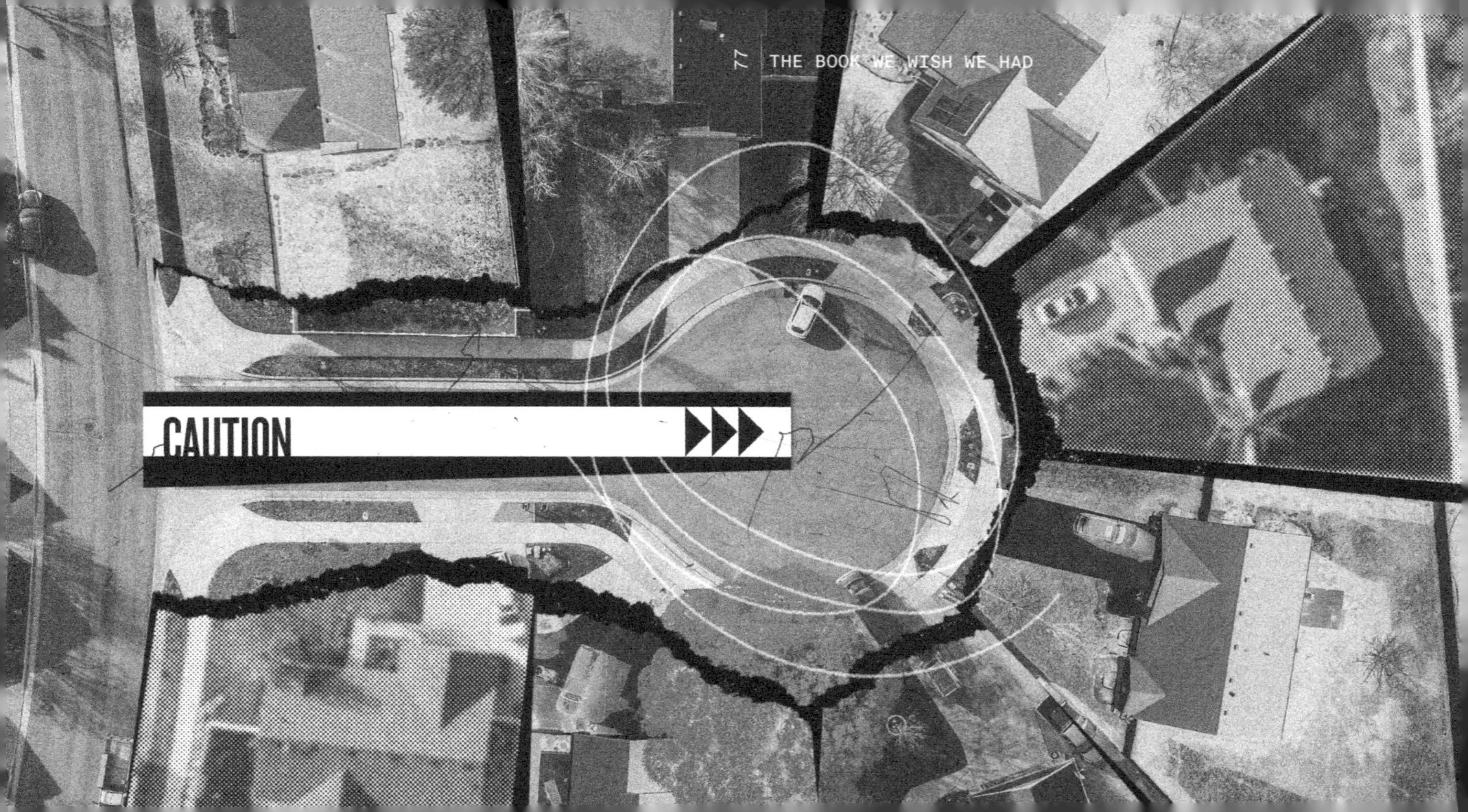
CAUTION

“Tough client” is redundant.

You won't always like what clients do, say, or decide, but it's their money. You have three options:

1. Get over it.
2. Find a way to work around it. (There's always a way.)
3. Refuse to work on the business.

Default to #3 too often and it could lead to option #4: Find another job.

The beat poet.

While practicing for a pitch to one of the biggest tech companies on the planet—a critical piece of business for the agency—I was repeatedly told by well-intentioned senior execs at the agency that my presentation style was too this or too that. At one point, I was even told I sounded "like a beat poet." My emotions ranged from embarrassment to frustration to anger to apathy. By the time the pitch arrived, I felt more ill-prepared than when we started rehearsing. We ultimately lost the pitch. I took the loss personally.

After beating myself up about it, self-assessing, and soul-searching (in that order), I realized something. While doing my best to adopt the presentation styles of others, I had lost something important along the way: me. Subsequently, my part in the presentation came across as muted, out-of-step, and disingenuous.

That challenging experience taught me something important when it comes to presentations: Be yourself. Along with knowing the audience in the room, knowing what points to make, and knowing what marks to hit, also know that it's best to do it all in your own personal style.

There will be times when more experienced colleagues try to script you, telling you to present proposals or concepts their way rather than yours. Always consider the advice—that's how you learn—but be cautious about losing your own personal style in the process. Trying to copy someone else's mannerisms, approach, and dynamics can make you appear disingenuous or rehearsed. It's tough to sell anything if people don't believe you.

Practice **Shoshin.**

In 2007, Microsoft's then-CEO Steve Ballmer famously proclaimed the iPhone would never "get any significant market share—no chance." To date, more than 2 billion iPhones have been sold. Ballmer would have been wise to practice Shoshin, a Zen Buddhist term meaning "beginner's mind." Practitioners are encouraged to remain curious and filled with wonder, particularly with things they do regularly.

Renowned cellist Yo Yo Ma said he always approaches the instrument "like a child playing for the first time." Amazon founder Jeff Bezos says, "Every day at Amazon is Day One." (Nothing like a trillion-dollar market cap to prove the power of Shoshin.)

It's not easy playing the role of a perpetual beginner. People will scoff at you, even scold you. Your own inner ego may rise against you. (See: *Ego Kills*) But that's how you know you're on the right path. Reject the this-is-how-we-always-do-it arguments, renounce outdated stereotypes, burn the cherished company playbook, and collar your ego. Only then can you discover new possibilities.

No student should become the master without also remaining a student.

Go **hippo hunting.**

Brands and companies are obsessed with awareness. Awareness is empty. You may be aware of the people on the sidewalk, but you'll forget them two steps later. What companies should be seeking is something more meaningful and lasting: **being remembered.** And that requires an emotional connection.

The brain's hippocampus plays a role in making our memories stick. Broadly speaking, it slaps an emotional stamp on key experiences so we don't forget them. That's why you remember your first love, the car accident you had, or those front-row concert seats.

Neuroscientist Antonio Damasio, head of the USC Brain and Creativity Institute, discovered something extraordinary while studying emotions. People with damage to the emotional centers of their brain could not make even the most basic decisions, such as whether to have a chicken or turkey sandwich for lunch, because there's no deep logic involved in that decision. Instead, the emotional centers of the brain kick in and tip the decision one way or the other. "We are not thinking machines that feel," concludes Damasio. "Rather, we are feeling machines that think."

Brands spend too much time spouting forgettable facts and functions at people and practically no time trying to make more moving, meaningful, and memorable connections with them. If you really want to make a lasting impression, go hippo hunting.

Get uncomfortable.

No creative session can survive the suffocating weight of sacred cows, policy police, and timeworn taboos. People must be free to say the unspeakable, consider the unimaginable and go to forbidden places. There is no room for self-censorship when seeking new ideas.

Often, the whole point of an unforgettable idea is to make people feel uncomfortable, or as Banksy explained, "Art should comfort the disturbed and disturb the comfortable."

If Nike had used golden boy Drew Brees in its 2018 "Dream Crazy" ad rather than the controversial and polarizing Colin Kaepernick, no one would have cared. It would have been . . . comfortable.

But getting uncomfortable is not for everyone. If you are worried that some of the topics discussed during a creative session might offend people, warn the group ahead of time. Explain that some uncomfortable topics might be explored and controversial comments might be made during the meeting. Those who might feel put off or offended are welcome to opt out without judgment.

Remember, if clients love everything you do, you're not pushing hard enough.

Break the brief.

It's not uncommon to have five to ten agencies in a pitch, maybe more. During these ridiculous Best-of-Show competitions, you have two choices: Pull out of the lineup or break the brief. Both have merit.

Pulling out of the pageant is a woefully underused option in the agency world. The win rates are dismal—especially when the incumbent agency is in the running. (Where are the numbercrunchers when you need them?) Companies that bring in a parade of agencies are either satisfying internal procurement procedures or just looking to see what's out there. What do they have to lose? It costs them nothing.

Respectfully opting out of these cattle calls sends an important message to your team and to the prospective client: We are about valued client relationships, not talentshow competitions. (See: *Leave When They Want You to Stay*)

Breaking the brief is a worthy option too. You still deliver against the core challenge in the brief, but you do it in a way that defies convention and makes heads pop. You present something so ambitious and daring it goes beyond the limitations of the brief, stealing the spotlight from all the other agencies. If you do decide to use this approach, keep asking yourself: "There are nine other agencies working on the same assignment. Did they land in the same place we did?" **Go big or stay home.**

Fail bravely.

There are more than 1 billion pithy musings, anecdotes, and poetic excerpts of prose on Google about the long-term advantages of failure. So why does everyone avoid it like a colonoscopy? **Because it's shitty.**

When your idea tanks and the time and money you invested in a project is lost, the last thing you want to hear is "failures are finger posts on the road to achievement." Bite me, C. S. Lewis. Still, the fallout of failure is real . . . but it ain't permanent. You will survive. Just ask Lady Gaga, Steve Jobs, Bill Belichick, or Oprah Winfrey–all of whom were fired.

Failure is the one situation where your imagination works against you, conjuring up images of all the potential repercussions of that failure–getting fired, losing credibility, being publicly embarrassed. That kind of mind-play serves no purpose other than to fill you with unhealthy anxiety and destroy your confidence.

It's okay to be down and reflective–self-assessment is a tool for growth–just don't wallow in it. It's wasted energy. As they say in Silicon Valley: Fail fast and fix it.

Order the damn hamburger.

Kim, our feisty and beloved finance director, was sadly and slowly dying of cancer. It was not only an agonizing blow to her own family, but her work family as well.

I coaxed Kim to dinner one night in the hopes of cheering her up. Before long we were laughing, with Kim showing hints of her old playful spirit. As we sat looking at the menu deciding what to eat, I agonized over the fattening hamburger I wanted to order, weighing the delight in eating it against the regrettable fat content.

"Jeremy," Kim calmly interrupted. "Do you want that hamburger?"

"Well, yeah," I replied, sheepishly.

"Then order the damn hamburger," she said with a weary smile.

Kim ultimately lost her battle with cancer, but not before leaving me an important lesson about how silly our "problems" are in life. Most of the time, the anxieties and fears we feel are nothing more than melodramatic manifestations created in our minds. You will survive every failed project, each minor or major misstep, and all the embarrassing moments in between. So . . . order the damn hamburger.

Thank you, Kim. You are missed.

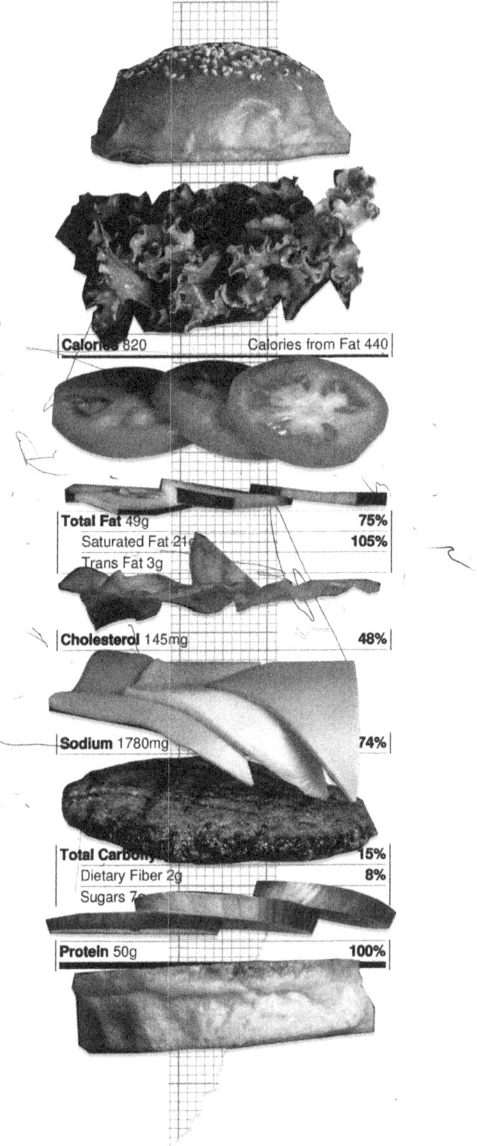

Calories from Fat 440
Total Fat 49g
75%
105%
Trans Fat 3g
Cholesterol 145mg
48%
Sodium 1780mg
74%
15%
Dietary Fiber 2g
8%
Protein 50g
100%

Ego kills.

During one of my guest lectures at UCLA, a student asked, "During meetings, do you feel like you're the most creative person in the room?" I was as surprised by the question as he was by my response. "Actually, it's the complete opposite," I said. "I feel like I'm probably one of the least creative people in the room."

Believing you're the best in the room doesn't make you more confident; it makes you more vulnerable. In his book *High Performance Habits: How Extraordinary People Become That Way*, best-selling author Brandon Burchard shares extensive research showing that the #1 trap successful people can fall into is a "superiority complex," or believing they are smarter than everyone else. As soon as you think you know it all, Burchard warns, it makes you close-minded to alternative opinions or new possibilities. (Remember to embrace Shoshin, the beginner's mind.)

Top-ranked poker player Daniel Negreanu sums it up best. "When you feel like you've got this game mastered and you've got nothing left to learn," says the six-time World Series of Poker champion, "that's the exact point where everyone else starts to surpass you."

Go there.

Save your breath, we've heard all the tired arguments before: "They'll never buy it." "This makes it look like we didn't follow the brief." "This might turn them off to us permanently."

In the hundreds upon hundreds of presentations we've done over the years, never has a client said, "We didn't pick you because one of the ideas you presented was just too bold, exciting, and imaginative."

When presenting ideas, be sure to showcase a range of creative thinking. It's okay to share concepts that are familiar but still creative, as long as you also share some that are breathtaking in design and daring, pushing the client beyond his or her comfort zone. If you only share safe and familiar ideas, they will come to believe that's all you can do. And they can get that anywhere.

In short, presenting concepts is not an either/or proposition. It's not a choice between sharing some bold ideas or some safe ideas. Present both. Don't hold back only to have to hear: "This is nice, but we were looking for something really different and breakthrough."

Miracle on Rodeo.

Years ago, prior to the holidays, a video company was looking to generate some last-minute buzz for their portable video game called The Nomad. There was only one catch: "We only have $1,500," admitted the client. "That's probably barely enough for a photo shoot."

Most would have rightfully declined the challenge. But I was already wondering how much a camel cost.

"Because it's The Nomad," I riffed. "What if we had a Santa ride a camel down Rodeo Drive with a sign that reads, 'Nomad'?"

The client sat silent for a moment. "Can we even get a camel?" he finally asked.

"It's Hollywood," I countered. "We'll get a camel."

He hedged. "Is Beverly Hills just going to let us ride a camel down Rodeo Drive?"

Good question.

"If you do that," the snooty Beverly Hills City Commission director said on the phone the next day, "we'll not only arrest you, we'll sue you." I could see the headlines already: "Beverly Hills Sues Camel-Riding Santa Holding Nomad Sign." Loved it. I secured a camel from Animals 'R Us (only in LA), and at 6 a.m. the following day, I stood with the slobbering animal in a Beverly Hills parking lot waiting for my mall Santa—who never showed. Kringle bastard.

A half-hour later, I found myself in an over-sized Santa suit lumbering down Rodeo Drive on the back of a camel. "Grab the neck reins! Grab the neck reins!" shouted the anxious camel trainer below. "I can't see the mother fwphing neck rwphs!" I yelled back, spitting the Santa beard from my mouth. By then, two Beverly Hills cruisers were on my tail—or my camel's tail.

"You're done. Done!" yelled one of the cops, pulling out his ticket book. Before I could even hear the cop tell me what law I had broken by riding a camel on Rodeo Drive, a miracle occurred.

"Let him go! It's Christmas!" yelled a mom from a Range Rover.

"Give him a break! Santa's a celebrity!" yelled a guy in a Porsche.

"Free Santa! Free Santa!" shouted another woman, pumping her fist.

Horns everywhere were honking, blasting, beeping. Sensing the growing movement, the cop leaned in close. "You've got TWO MINUTES to get this thing out of here," he hissed, as the news copters hovered overhead. Move over, George Bailey! There's a new angelic truth: Every time a horn honks, a

Santa's ass is saved!

A week later, my phone rang. It was the snooty director from the Beverly Hills City Commission. "Heh, heh," chuckled my former adversary. "The stores on Rodeo Drive experienced some record sales because of all the news attention your little stunt created the other day," he said, sheepishly. "Are you planning anything next year?"

Honk, honk!

Find a **conspirator.**

It's surprising how many agencies are afraid of clients. They worry that an offbeat idea might anger or frustrate them. "We don't want the client to think we're not listening to them," is the common agency cry. Well, maybe you shouldn't be listening to them. Maybe they should be listening to you? (See: *There's a Difference Between Client Service and Client Servitude*)

I am always amused by companies that come to any agency explaining that, over the last several years, their market share shrank, their brand lost relevance, and their sales tumbled. Then, agencies immediately set out to create something the client will like, trying to think just like they do. Uh, isn't that kind of thinking what got them in this predicament in the first place? Shouldn't we be doing the opposite, or at least something different?

"That could put the account at risk," comes back the reply. So, many agencies often default to ideas they know are not as strong simply to keep the client happy.

Ironically, the result is the same—clients who are unhappy because the creative isn't making the impact they wanted. And what do you say then? "Yeah, we didn't think the creative would work, but we were afraid to tell you"? Clients *pay* for your opinion. Give it to them. Sometimes, it's your job to save clients (or bosses) from themselves.

To make it easier, find a fellow conspirator on the client side, an undercover accomplice who conspires with you to get unconventional creative approved, who runs interference against fellow holdouts or naysayers, who gives you internal intel on how best to position your arguments and sell your ideas through.

Behind nearly every award-winning campaign is a hidden conspirator who helped make it happen.

Conference room consumers.

During a meeting at the corporate office of a major fast-food chain, we were presenting a series of campaigns aimed at consumers ages 18 to 24. It was a dismal meeting. One idea after another was shot down, deemed too racy, too risqué, or just too daring in general. It was apparent we had failed our creative assignment. But then something occurred to me. Looking around the room, I noted that everyone around the table was well over 30 years old, with some in their 50s.

As the group proceeded to pick apart yet another idea, I interrupted the slaughter. "It's worth noting that none of us around this table is between the ages of 18 and 24," I observed. "So, while we may think talking about drinking, drugs, hooking up, and loud music is inappropriate, our target calls it Saturday."

To the company's credit, the following week they hosted a brainstorm in some rented office space amidst the bars, nightclubs, and music venues on the Sunset Strip. There's nothing like the sounds of partying, pulsating music, horn-honking, and the scent of sativa to get the creative juices flowing.

Don't let "conference room consumers" become your entire target audience. You could end up with a campaign that eleven people love . . . and 22 million twentysomethings hate.

Anticipate **the hate.**

A YouTube video entitled "Adopted girl and her mother discuss when they first met," features a delightful, rosy-cheeked child explaining in unbridled, heart-melting words just how much she loves her adoptive parents. It generated more than 7 million views and racked up 300,000+ likes. And nearly 4,000 dislikes. Thousands of people found something to hate about a little girl expressing unconditional love for her parents. Tough crowd.

No matter how hard you grind, how excited you are to share what you created, how overwhelmingly smart, positive, and powerful you believe it is, somebody is going to hate it. Expect that and accept it.

Trying to create something everyone will equally love and appreciate is like toiling over the design of a squirt gun that will put out a wildfire. It's wasted energy. If what you created is something you and your diverse team truly believe in and feel represents your best work, that's enough. And don't forget, creating something that has people taking different sides has the benefit of sparking discussion, buzz, and attention. Being hated is better than being completely ignored.

"If I make music and people hate it, you know, whatever," says singer-songwriter Billie Eilish. "I'll die someday and, one day, they will too."

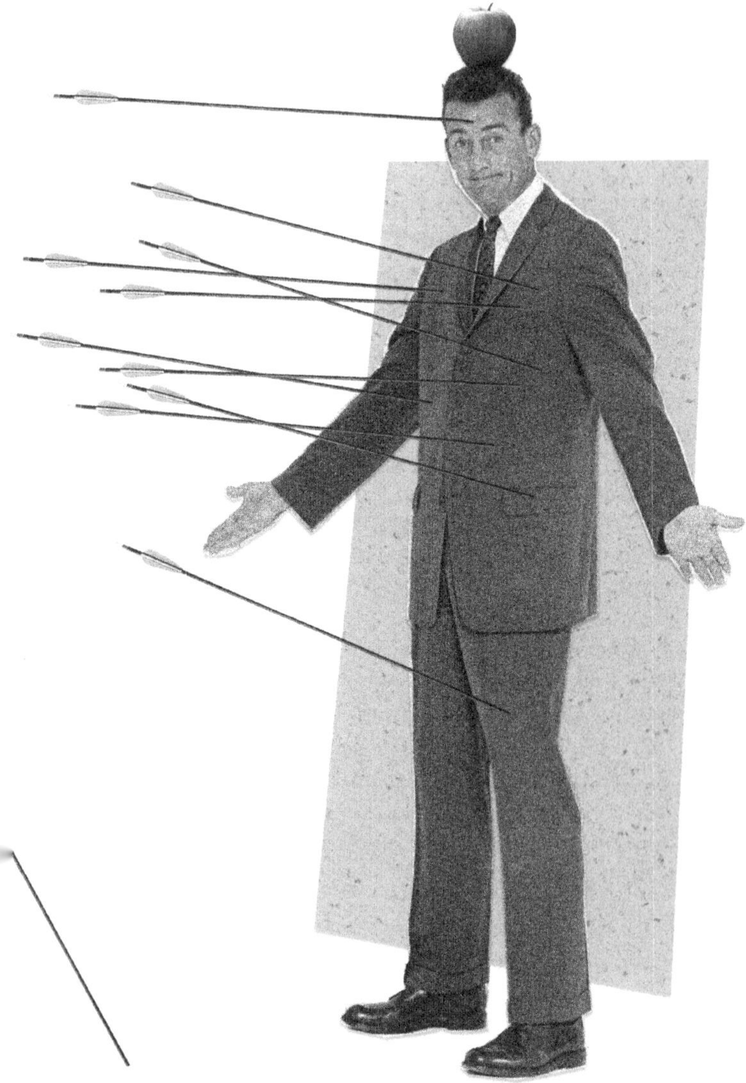

Filthy dirty martinis.

There's something to be said about the creative power of a few martinis and some cocktail napkins. Rollin King and Herb Kelleher's idea for a low-cost airline called Southwest, Brooke Runnette's idea for Shark Week, and Jay Park's idea for Facebook's new data center were all mapped out on cocktail napkins. In fact, I sat and watched during a Hollywood lunch as screenwriting legend Joe Eszterhas wrote a script idea on a napkin for which he was ultimately paid $4 million.

According to our own personal research, the best thinking occurs after two martinis (Ketel One, three olives). Never three martinis, or the next day you'll likely wake to an email note from yourself that reads like a coded CIA message: "Jar campaign, strat angle for." (Never did figure that one out.)

If our own research isn't good enough for you, take it from the Newt/Judge Experiment that involved eighteen advertising creatives split into two groups. Researchers conducted two three-hour-long brainstorm sessions where one group drank alcohol and the other group drank only water. Not only did the alcohol-drinking group generate more ideas, but of the five concepts the judges selected as the best, four of them came from the tipsy team.

Note: If you're going to drink while ideating, take a ride service home. Ideate responsibly.

You go, **you get.**

The most powerful connections in business are made face-to-face. While the convenience, affordability, and time-saving advantages of technology make it tempting to present concepts remotely, always push for an in-person pitch. You're stacking the deck in your favor.

According to a *Forbes* survey of 760 business executives, 91 percent of them believe face-to-face meetings are more persuasive. There's also something to be said about the spontaneous discussions, introductions, and invitations that happen after in-person presentations that don't occur as much during virtual meetings or phone calls.

Go the extra mile to get the extra advantage.

Shout-out to Bob Molino.

Leave when they **want you to stay.**

American streetwear designer Don C once said in the midst of a creative session, "I want to leave while you want me to stay."

Taking every minute of allotted time (and then some) during a presentation, lingering until the client must go, or hovering outside an office to talk to a client–these actions all send one overriding and unflattering message: **desperation.**

Don't hang around like a starstruck kid waiting for an autograph. Say your piece, make an impression, and move on. You have better things to do because, frankly, you are in demand.

Don't be a **brilliant jerk.**

No matter how good you are, if your attitude sucks then your time here is limited. Companies literally can't afford your bad attitude. Consider these findings from business consulting firm Leadership IQ:

- 87 percent of employees feel like changing jobs when working with people who have a bad attitude.
- 93 percent of workers say they're less productive when working with a bad attitude.
- 89 percent of new hires who fail within 18 months lose their jobs because of a bad attitude, not job performance.

One year, an edgy Netflix HR presentation highlighting the company's culture, work ethic, and performance expectations went viral. Included in the outlined policies was a pledge to never hire "brilliant jerks."

"Some companies tolerate them," said CEO Reed Hastings. "For us, the cost to effective teamwork is too high."

Don't be a brilliant jerk. Be a brilliant team player.

Know the **numbers.**

Follow the money. Don't chase it, but be sure to understand how your work generates revenue for the business. Build allegiances with key clients and important partners. Being connected to a valuable piece of client work is a form of body armor, bullet-proofing you from getting fired—or fired at. Become key to the operation, that person no one can do without. Ideas may be subjective, but contributions to the bottom line are 100 percent objective.

Buy a round or two—

on you.

Buying a round of drinks is an easy way to show appreciation. And it means even more when the round is on you, not the company.

On many occasions, colleagues ask me directly, "Is this on you or the company?" People want to know. Because there's a difference between a gesture that says, "I appreciate you" and one that says, "the company appreciates you." You would be surprised at the level of loyalty and respect simple gestures like this can create.

Beat back **bias.**

Years ago, Tony (not his real name) was the executive vice president of marketing at a national resort chain. He was extremely conservative, painfully formal, and largely humorless. As the chain grew, so did the marketing department, prompting Tony to hire more conservative, formal, and humorless marketers. The resulting ad campaigns had all the imagination of a rice cake. One entire photo shoot was scrapped because the models photographed around the pool were not wearing shoes or flip-flops. The marketing team considered this distasteful.

The executives all scratched their heads over the dismal performance of their campaigns. But like someone staring into the sun, they couldn't see the reason because they were blinded by it: unconscious bias. The team was designing campaigns that fit their own beliefs, their own preferences, their own dogma and doctrine. Subsequently, they were marketing to only one audience: people who were conservative, traditional, formal, and humorless.

Biases are like bad habits—we all have them, some worse than others. "Like it or not," says social psychologist Dr. Jennifer Eberhardt, "if you have a brain, you have bias." But left unchecked, Eberhardt warns, unconscious bias "can shackle us in place." Bias is creative kryptonite.

The first step toward beating back our own biases is recognizing them. Easier said than done. That's why it's important to surround yourself with a diverse team of people with opposing views, alternative opinions, and different life experiences. They will keep you honest—but only if the feedback chain remains free, open, and honest. Make sure it does.

Look around. Does everyone on your team look and sound like you? If so, mix it up before it takes you down.

Shoot straight.

Shoot straight—always—including and especially during performance conversations. If you sugarcoat feedback or tell little white lies to protect people's feelings, they'll never get any better. What's more, it makes you look weak and duplicitous.

Legendary Apple designer Jony Ive talks about the "brilliantly brutal" piece of feedback he once received from Steve Jobs. Ive had asked Jobs to be a little less harsh when delivering his critiques to the design team. Jobs surprised the earnest Ive. "You're just really vain," Ive recalls Jobs saying. "You want people to like you. And I'm surprised at you, because I thought you held the work up as most important, not how you believe you are perceived by other people." This made Ive "really cross." Mainly, he later admitted, because he knew Jobs was right.

It's true. Some execs just want to be liked, which can impair their judgment.

Once when working with a senior leader at an agency, he briefed us on some ideas he was seeking for a key client. Later, a young creative on our team sent him an email with some initial ideas and copied me. "Awesome, love it. Keep going!" the exec replied enthusiastically. I was surprised. The ideas seemed divergent from the briefing request. I called the exec to try to clarify. "Honestly, it was off," he said, under his breath. "But, you know, I didn't want to discourage him."

You can be positive and productive with your critiques, but not at the expense of honesty. Sending team members away excited and happy but ill-informed and misdirected helps no one.

Being a straight shooter helps ensure everyone hits the target.

Nemo resideo.

"Nemo resideo" is Latin for "leave no one behind." A U.S. military code of honor.

During SEAL team training, if one recruit fails a challenge the entire unit is punished because they did not work together to succeed. Navy SEALs believe selflessness is the most important element of a team. "Once the individuals in the group begin to act selflessly," explains one SEAL team instructor, "the goals of the entire team are achievable."

Form your own "leave no one behind" code and build a team that creates, works, celebrates, fights, defends, and wins together; a team that not only gives a shit about the work they do, but the people who do it.

Put on the **Med-Eng EOD.**

The Military Explosive Ordinance Disposal suit, also known as an EOD or Blast Suit, is designed to withstand the pressure of a bomb blast and flying debris moving as fast as 3,728 miles per hour. Great creative leaders should know when to wear it to absorb the irrational, explosive, and demoralizing changes to concepts.

It's your job to absorb the impact of potentially destructive feedback, mitigate the damage, keep your team motivated, and provide clear and constructive direction to move the project forward. If you let the blast hit your team, the shrapnel will tear down morale.

After working nearly 36 hours straight on a seemingly impossible challenge, the creative team and I sat, blurry eyed, in the conference room waiting (dreading?) to hear from the account lead what the client's reaction was to our ideas.

"He liked a *lot* of it," Leslie, the account lead said, excitedly, snapping us awake as she bounded into the room. "I think we can combine pieces of what we have, add a few things and get his buy-in." We were relieved. While it wasn't exactly a full-throated embrace of our concepts, at least he didn't *hate* them.

Or did he?

Months later, I discovered the client was, in fact, quite unhappy with our ideas, even questioning our creative capabilities.

Leslie, however, got him to admit that he actually liked bits and pieces of concepts, convincing him we could combine them and get to where we needed to be. (And we did.)

Had Leslie shared directly the raw and disparaging comments from the client, it would have served no other purpose than to completely demoralize the team, probably prompting some to refuse to work on the business.

Instead, Leslie strapped on her blast-ordinance gear and absorbed the cutting critique and flying vitriol. She not only saved the creative team from having to hear it, but she also saved the project in the process.

Oorah.

It's called **feedback** for a reason.

People ask more probing questions about their cooking than they do about their rejected ideas. "You didn't like the steak? Was it too rare? Overcooked? Did I add too much seasoning? Do you even like seasoning? Are you a vegetarian? How about fish instead?" But when people hear their concept got rejected, they act like a trapdoor will open if they ask one too many questions about why.

It's called feedback for a reason. You feed the clients something you think they'll like, they feed back to you their reaction so you can get closer to what they want in the next round. Without that collaborative process, nailing the creative assignment is like throwing darts over your shoulder.

Getting the right feedback is as much your responsibility as it is the client's. Ask lots of smart and pointed questions. What did they like most about the idea/design and why? What did they like least about it and why? Is there an example they can point to that represents what they're looking for? Is the idea you presented in the right ballpark or in the wrong city?

To encourage more detailed feedback, explain that the more specifics you get, the less time and money it will take to land on the right idea. Otherwise, you could find yourself serving up meaty concepts to a room full of vegans.

Get comfortable with **rejection.**

More than 500,000. That's the estimated number of ideas we have had rejected by bosses, clients, prospective clients, peers, colleagues, even each other.

People constantly ask, "What do you do when a client keeps rejecting your ideas?" There's only one answer: Pitch them more. The only other option is to give up, and everyone loses in that scenario. As a senior marketing executive at a large financial institution once explained to us, "You need to know that nine times out of ten we're going to turn down your ideas for some reason—but we still want the ideas." (Be sure you're in synch with what they want, however, or you're just wasting time.) Translation: Keep at it.

A 2020 Super Bowl commercial featuring Bruce Springsteen was the first one ever for the legendary rock star. For more than 40 years, he famously rejected any and all ideas from commercial companies and brands, doggedly protecting his down-home, Jersey-boy image. But that didn't stop Olivier Francois from trying.

Francois is the chief marketing officer at Stellantis, the automaker behind Jeep. For ten straight years, he pitched ideas and concepts to Springsteen's longtime manager, Jon Landau. "They would turn me down—always," says Francois. "I can't help but try to sell my ideas, [but] it never worked. It never worked." Until it did.

Springsteen liked the unity message behind one of the Jeep concepts and, just weeks before the Super Bowl, surprisingly agreed to do it. "It took me ten years to get him in, but once he was in, he was all in," Francois said.

Be persistent and patient. Eventually, if you listen, adjust, and remain dedicated to your craft, it pays off. Meanwhile, you're learning, creating, what-iffing all along the way.

Take credit.

Being humble and kind might make for a Grammy Award-winning country song, but in the work environment it can cost you. Be a team player, but not to the point where your value becomes blurred.

In a frenetic work environment, it's not uncommon for superiors to lose sight of who is contributing what. On occasion, you may be left out of the end credits list. Or worse, someone else might get credit for your work or thinking.

When appropriate (such as during reviews or casual conversations) let the right people know your creative contributions. But be careful not to sound impudent, egotistical, or self-centered. Keep it focused on your ability to actively participate and collaborate, doing your part to help the team. Also, when sharing an original thought or idea with someone via email, consider copying another person or two. It's a great way to keep your team in the loop while naturally reinforcing the origin of the idea.

Once you "own" the idea, however, be prepared to defend it or take the heat if things go south. A great idea has many parents, but a bad one is always an orphan.

We're all **Imposters.**

Do you secretly believe you're not as capable as your colleagues? That you are at times faking it in meetings and will eventually be revealed as a fraud?

Join the club.

Up to 82 percent of us experience something psychologists call impostor syndrome. "I still have a little impostor syndrome," says Michelle Obama. "It doesn't go away, that feeling you shouldn't take me that seriously. What do I know? We all have doubts in our abilities, about our power."

Imagine experiencing the nagging self-doubt of impostor syndrome in the middle of painting a mural five stories high. International street artist Fintan Magee admits it happens.

"The only time it's an issue," he cautions, "is if it stops you from creating because you are telling yourself, 'I can't do this.'"

The evil inner voice of impostor syndrome can be particularly chatty early in your career, scoffing at and second-guessing your abilities and creative choices. Just know that it happens to nearly everyone, including your boss.

Ultimately, we're all just making it up.

Don't tell Disney
how to Disney.

Don't try to out-brand the brand people at long-standing companies. You'll either turn them off or piss them off. Instead, serve as their provocateur, the what-iffer, the why-notter. Be the listener, the dot-connector. Provide them the thinking they can't see because they've been too close to it too long.

Clients are often so familiar with their brand or company that they become short-sighted experts. As an outsider, your greatest value comes from being free from all the preconceived notions, prior failures, unwritten rules, and outdated beliefs. Everyone is already thinking about what's best for the brand; it's your job to think of what's next for the brand.

And remember, if your client loves everything you do or say, you're not pushing hard enough.

Practice **brutal simplicity.**

If you can't summarize your idea in a tweet, it's too complicated.

Screenwriters crystalize their scripts in a one-sentence logline, 25 to 50 words that succinctly capture the essence of their story. Loglines are used to entice busy producers, studio execs, and directors into wanting to hear more.

Name the iconic movies behind these loglines:

1. A young janitor at M.I.T. has a gift for mathematics but needs help from a psychologist to find direction in his life.
2. Two imprisoned men bond over several years, finding solace and eventual redemption through acts of common decency.
3. A cowboy doll is profoundly threatened and jealous when a new spaceman figure supplants him as top toy in a boy's room.
4. A young Black man is invited to visit his White girlfriend's parents' estate and soon realizes the family has a very dark history.

Can you turn your idea into a logline that people simply must see or hear more about? (See: *Write Amazing Sentences*)

Stop idea stacking.

Stacking is when a single idea gets buried under an avalanche of bells, whistles, gadgets, and things. It starts to look and sound like an infomercial: "But wait! There's more! We'll even throw in this shock-resistant watch, heat-resistant hiking socks, and a hand-painted coffee mug!"

Idea stacking most often occurs when a concept isn't meaningful, compelling, or captivating enough on its own, so people start throwing in a celebrity, a charity donation, a popular influencer, an AI device, a billboard, a drone display, a pop-up event, the Metaverse . . . in a misguided attempt to make it interesting and newsworthy.

If you sense your team is starting to stack, stop the madness. Assess the situation, going back to the beginning if necessary, to identify where the idea went off track in the first place.

Stacking poker chips–good. Stacking ideas–not good.

DISCO

Stop **comment stacking,** too.

Pick your moment to share. And when you do, make it count.

Once, in a meeting with a major retailer, a top executive sat silently for almost the entire meeting. I began to wonder why she was even there. Toward the end, she spoke. Not only did she crystalize into one simple notion the strategy we had been struggling with for almost an hour, but she also shared a mic-dropping idea that left the room speechless.

When participating in meetings, don't just say something to test your voice box. Instead, make it count. Continuing to add your two cents only to try to prove your market value is a waste. Worse, it can kill the flow of a discussion, a presentation, or an idea.

While it's okay to practice your in-meeting discussion skills during less formal team gatherings, for client meetings where big ideas and money are at stake, hold that thought–unless you honestly believe it could change the course of the meeting.

In the end, speaking up is better than saying nothing. (See: *Don't Be Irrelevant*) Just try to send up more winners than losers.

Master the **side hustle.**

A side hustle is what happens when an outside passion turns into potential profit.

Let's face it, not everyone lands their dream job. In fact, when starting out, most of us aren't even sure what our dream job would look like. Talent manager Julie Rice and real estate agent Elizabeth Cutler discovered they had a surprising passion for spin classes. They started their own cycling studio on the side, hoping to make a few extra bucks. Ten years later they sold SoulCycle for $180 million. And Ava DuVernay was still working full-time at her public relations job when she started side hustling as a director. Nothing like a side hustle that leads to an Academy Award Best Picture nomination for *Selma*. DuVernay is quick to point out, however, that "hustling" doesn't always mean fast.

"There is something in our culture that says your dream or the thing you're pursuing has to happen immediately and all at once," explains the filmmaker. "I just embraced the idea that this was going to be a gradual exploration of the thing I was interested in—making films—and gave myself permission to go slowly."

Side hustles don't always lead to riches or a star on the Hollywood Walk of Fame, but there are other benefits. Feeding your passions outside of work can actually keep you feeling more fulfilled, engaged, and inspired at your main job. And you'll be surprised just how many of the learnings, experiences, and influences gathered during your side hustle can actually be applied at work, making you even better.

Remember, though, don't let your side hustle overshadow your responsibilities at your main gig, or else you might just find yourself hustling for a new job. Find the proper balance.

Bounce.

Staying at the same job for many years may seem like the loyal, honorable, and stable thing to do, but it can also hurt you financially. Research suggests that remaining at the same company for even two years can impact your lifetime earnings by 50 percent or more. It stagnates your growth, stifles your thinking, and narrows your perspective. The more you jump, the more you learn, the more you make.

If the thought of leaving is on your mind, this is a good time to turn to a mentor. Ask someone you trust if it's time to move on. Most importantly, be honest with yourself. What are you running after . . . or running from? Are you leaving because of a personality conflict with a colleague or boss? Because you want more money? Because you aren't growing professionally? Because you want to experience a new city or career path? Knowing that answer will help determine your next move.

Bottom line: If you love where you are, great. Just make sure you're staying because you are happy and inspired, not because you're comfortable.

Stay in touch.

Stay in touch with former clients, colleagues, bosses, students, mentors, freelancers, and other work associates. As you or they move on, someone in your loose network might just end up being your next great new hire, client, outside collaborator, or even business partner.

Years ago, a bright, ambitious young woman was hired as our intern. We kept her involved, spent time teaching her things, and gave her opportunities that even mid-level people at other agencies don't normally get. She loved the challenges and the people. A few years later, she landed a job at Toyota, remembered how well we treated her, and returned the favor. She championed us to her boss who happened to be in the middle of an agency search. A month later we were pitching the marketing team at Toyota.

Relax, it's just a career.

What seems like a life-or-death business crisis today is going to seem silly a few weeks from now.

To keep things in perspective, I save old notebooks and digital documents containing urgent notes and reminders I made to myself during important meetings and calls. I later read all the critical notations, such as "Video must be done NO LATER THAN JUNE 16, NO EXTENSIONS!" I then reflect on how imperative, even potentially career-ending, they all seemed at the time. And now . . . not so much.

Create your own reminders of challenges overcome or crises survived. They will help put things in perspective for you when you're mired in the next must-get-it-right-or-else assignment.

Five words to the 21-year-old you.

A fun "parlor game" we sometimes play with colleagues and clients involves a time-travel quirk that allows you to go back into time and quickly share just five words of advice with the 21-year-old you. Based on what you know now, what would your five words be?

Jeremy's five words to his younger self would be: "Everything changes, good and bad."

Matt's five words of advice would be: "Your relationships will be everything."

What are your five words?

Nothing but time.

Being a mentor costs you nothing but time. And the reward is immeasurable.

Remember how hard you worked to create opportunities for yourself? Create those opportunities for the next generation. Leave your team in better hands than when you started. Take extra time to help people. Pass along the wealth of learnings and wisdom you acquired from your own mentors and life experiences, including and especially the failures.

Do it right and you will ultimately be creating a symbiotic flow of learning between you and your mentees, allowing everyone to continue to evolve and grow.

Embrace the spirit of this book and be the mentor you wish you had.

Dearest Mason,

Be thoughtful of others. Respect everyone as singular. And work really hard.

Every day, take time to appreciate what you have versus what you do not, and I promise you'll always have enough.

Love,
Your Dad

Breathe.

Years ago, my brother-in-law Denny was stricken with ALS, a progressive neurodegenerative disease that ultimately causes respiratory failure. It is a slow, suffocating death.

In just three years, Denny went from a tough, rock-'n'-roll-loving, semitruck-driving dude covered in tattoos to a gaunt, frail, failing figure receiving home hospice care. The guy who never backed away from a fight was in a fight for his life—and he fought the whole way. Even when he could no longer speak, his eyebrows "danced" to Van Halen's "Won't Get Fooled Again," as he mouthed the words he could no longer sing aloud: "We'll be fighting in the streets/With our children at our feet."

While visiting Denny one afternoon, I sat quietly with him watching TV. He lay there, motionless in his living room hospital bed that was a tangle of tubes and cords. Suddenly, he wanted to say something. Slowly—heroically—he nudged his BiPAP mask below his mouth. I leaned in, assuming he needed something urgent—water, food, help. He closed his eyes, summoned what little strength he had, and spoke. "You forget," he whispered, stopping a moment to gather his final bit of energy, "how good it is . . . to breathe." I never forgot those words.

Like all of us, over the years Denny had worried about paying bills, raising kids, keeping his spouse and family safe, and just navigating life. Now his entire focus—his moment-to-moment imperative—was centered on something the rest of us take for granted: a simple breath.

Denny ultimately surrendered to his illness, but not before bestowing upon me an invaluable life lesson. No matter how traumatic your day at work, how discouraged you may get, or how hopeless your career may seem at times, just take a deep breath . . . and remember that you can.

Here's to my sister and all the heroic caregivers out there.

A coffee I.V., an ashtray piled with cigarettes, and a corner office choking with smoke. I was in the office of Doug Buemi, a renegade executive leading one of the most successful offices at the world's largest PR agency. I was as impressed as I was frightened.

Doug worked 24/7, drank giant martinis, and read Charles Bukowski. His vocabulary was voluminous. Almost daily he would use a word I didn't know. He was irreverent about work, clients, people, and life. His ability to dissect a brand was almost creepy. I once watched him during a meeting write a tagline on a napkin and casually slide it over to the client. "Did you just come up with this?" asked the client, dumbfounded. Doug shrugged.

I was lucky enough to work alongside Doug for nearly 20 years, including when he owned his own agency. I absorbed his wisdom, his unapologetic creativity, his uncompromising integrity, and his penchant for risk-taking. (In 2005, at age 50, he sold his home in Los Angeles, gave away most of what he owned, got a tattoo, and moved to China—a place he had never even visited.) "I've always wanted to be an interesting man from an exotic land," he said. In less than a year, he won a chunk of the Ford business—a relatively early PR pioneer in the burgeoning Chinese market.

More than 25 years later, Doug remains my mentor, providing perspectives on everything from politics to poets, retail to real estate, and cooking to cryptocurrency. My career was shaped by his influence. So, in the unwritten law of mentorship, I pledged to pass along what I had learned.

Thanks, Dougie.

Jeremy

As a marketer with more than 25 years of international agency experience, Jeremy has worked for (or against) the world's biggest brands. His candid creative assessments and unapologetic boundary-pushing have been known to make more than a few clients uncomfortable—the exact point of entry for original ideas.

It's not something that can be assigned. It happens when you least expect it. You can actively search for it, but luck never hurts either.

I met Jeremy Baka while I was tending bar during college at a restaurant in Dana Point, unsure of what to do or where to go with my PR and Advertising degree from Chapman University. At least at the bar, I could pull in some extra dough and meet people. And one evening, as if on cue, in walked Jeremy, Sir Chief Creative Guy, from a big international marketing agency.

Jeremy ordered a "Frankie Blue Eyes." I promised to buy him that Jack Daniels if he swore to never order it that way again. We continued to banter throughout the evening, when he surprised me by asking what I wanted to do for a living. I told him I hadn't decided, but probably something in either PR or advertising. "You're going to shit yourself when you hear what I do for a living," Jeremy said, as he dropped me his card. I sent him an email a couple days later.

After a string of interviews, I found myself working for an international agency. Jeremy didn't have a reason to give a damn, but he looked out for me anyway. He lifted me up and I made sure not to let him down. We clicked creatively. Before long we were developing cool, edgy programs that tested client comfort zones.

Having a great mentor was (is) the most important reason for my success in this industry. I had a confidante that inspired me, listened to me, chopped me down and built me back up, dissected the decisions, focused me on the things that mattered, displayed a tenacious work ethic, and provided a strategic roadmap for the parts of my professional career that didn't yet have one. He was an example of how to treat people. How to take care of people. How to give a shit.

Thanks, Jeremy.

Matt

Southern California born and bred, Matt founded and leads the Strategy & Communications group at NVE Experience Agency. He has 15+ years of global agency experience and brand leadership from developing award-winning campaigns and culture-led marketing strategies for many of the world's most interesting brands. Matt and his wife Nicki (Jeremy was their wedding officiant) live in Sherman Oaks with their son, Mason.

Author photo by GRO Creative

The Book We Wish We Had

Made in the USA
Middletown, DE
30 August 2023

37662288R00093